W9-AAX-434

AMPHIBIANS

A TRUE BOOK

by
Melissa Stewart

Children's Press®
A Division of Grolier Publishing
New York London Hong Kong Sydney
Danbury, Connecticut

The webbed toes on this European frog's back feet make it easier for the frog to swim.

Content Consultants
Jan Jenner, Ph.D.
Jim Van Abbema, Ph.D.

Author's Dedication
For my editor and friend,
Julie Gillispie

The photograph on the cover shows two red-eyed tree frogs. The photograph on the title page shows a pair of fire salamanders.

Library of Congress Cataloging-in-Publication Data

Stewart, Melissa.
  Amphibians / by Melissa Stewart.
      p. cm. — (A true book)
  Includes bibliographical references and index.
  Summary: Describes the basic behavior, physical traits, and life cycles of amphibians.
  ISBN: 0-516-22037-3 (lib. bdg.)   0-516-25950-4 (pbk.)
    1. Amphibians—Juvenile literature. [1. Amphibians.] I. Title. II. Series.
  QL644.2.S745 2001
  597.8—dc21   99-057541
                                                                          CIP
                                                                          AC

Contents

Bullfrogs (top) are usually green to greenish-brown, and they often have gold or brown eyes. If you visit a limestone cave in the eastern United States, you might see a cave salamander (bottom) like this one.

What Is an Amphibian?

If you visit a small pond in the summer, you might see a giant bullfrog leap into the water. If you walk through the woods on a rainy afternoon, you might notice a brightly colored salamander scurry under a fallen log. Frogs and salamanders belong to a group of animals called amphibians (am-FI-bee-uhnz).

This group also includes a strange animal called a caecilian (si-SIL-yen). A caecilian looks more like a giant earthworm than a frog or a salamander. Most caecilians are about 12 inches (30 centimeters) long, but they can range from 7 to 54 inches (18 to 137 cm) long. They have no legs and are nearly blind.

Caecilians live in warm, moist areas, such as rain forests in Central America.

Caecilians spend their lives hidden underground in the moist soil of tropical forests. They eat worms, insects, and small lizards.

What do frogs, salamanders, and caecilians have in common? All amphibians have a backbone and moist, smooth skin. An amphibian's backbone supports its body and helps it move. Your backbone does the same jobs.

This flatwoods salamander's black-and-gray skin is moist and shiny.

Like most frogs, this tree frog's skin is covered with mucus.

All amphibians take in oxygen from the air through their thin skin and the lining of their mouths and throats. Some amphibians breathe through lungs like people do. Most amphibians produce a thick, slippery liquid called mucus. Mucus keeps an amphibian's skin moist, so it does not dry out.

There are about 3,200 kinds of amphibians on Earth. Most are less than 6 inches

The Chinese giant salamander weighs about 60 pounds (27 kilograms) and lives in fast-moving mountain streams.

(15 cm) long and weigh less than a box of animal crackers. The smallest frog in the world can sit on a person's thumbnail. The largest amphibian, the Chinese giant salamander, can be as long as a man is tall.

Most animals hide from their enemies, but many frogs and salamanders have bright colors that catch a predator's attention. When a hungry predator takes a bite of the amphibian, it gets a big surprise. An amphibian has glands in its skin that produce a bad-tasting liquid.

Away!

Some amphibians produce a liquid so poisonous that it kills predators immediately. But most of the time, the predator spits the amphibian out. The predator will remember the bad taste and not make the same mistake twice. The next time it sees an amphibian with brilliant red, orange, or blue skin, the predator will stay away.

Hot and Cold

Your body temperature is usually about 98.6 degrees Fahrenheit (37 degrees Celsius). Your body works hard to stay at this temperature. If you get too hot, your body sweats. If you get too cold, your body shivers. Scientists call this warm blooded.

This tomato frog is cooling down in a shady forest.

An amphibian is cold blooded. Its body does not work to stay at a constant temperature. Instead, an amphibian sits in the sun when it needs to warm up. It moves to a shady spot when it needs to cool down.

The wood frog can live in very cold weather. Amazingly, it can freeze as solid as an ice cube and stay frozen for 2 weeks or more.

At night, when the sun sets and the air temperature drops, an amphibian's body slows down. Amphibians that live in places with cold winters hibernate in underground burrows or at the bottom of ponds. While a wood frog hibernates, its breathing and heartbeat slow down. It survives all winter on fat stored inside its body.

Amphibians that live in places with very dry and hot

summers estivate (S-ti-vate). Estivate means that the amphibian rests underground to stay cool.

Spadefoot toads that live in deserts in the southwestern United States estivate. They remain underground most of the year. During a short rainy season, the toads burst out of their burrows and spend their days crowded in small pools and puddles. This is when the toads mate and

Spadefoot toads are active during the rainy season.

produce young. When the water disappears, so do the spadefoots.

A Double Life

The word "amphibian" comes from two Greek words—*amphi* means "double" and *bios* means "life." Many amphibians do lead a kind of double life. They spend the first part of their life in the water and the second part of their life on land.

This photograph shows a newly hatched spotted salamander larva (right) and an egg that is about to hatch (left). The larva has a long tail and no legs.

Young amphibians hatch from eggs laid in the water or on wet ground. The eggs are surrounded by a slippery jelly that tastes bad to most

These tadpoles have developed back legs.

predators. Young frogs and
salamanders are called larvae
(LAR-vay). Some people also
call young frogs tadpoles.

Larvae look like fat little fish. Each one has a long tail and no legs. Larvae breathe air through gills—just like fish.

After a few weeks, the young begin to grow legs and breathe with their lungs. The tails of the frogs disappear. Soon the young amphibians come out of the water.

The series of changes that an amphibian goes through to become an adult is called metamorphosis (me-ta-MOAR-fo-sis).

This bullfrog is calling for a mate. Each type of frog has its own mating call.

The next spring most amphibians will return to the pond or wetland where they hatched and grew into adults. Have you ever heard a frog "singing?" That sound is a male calling for a female. When she hears it, she follows the song until she finds the male.

After the frogs mate, the female will lay eggs.

A Look at Frogs

Most frogs have a huge mouth with a long tongue, bulging eyes on the top of their head, circular eardrums, and four legs. A frog uses its tongue to catch insects and its long, powerful back legs for jumping. Most frogs live in warm parts of the world, but two

A painted belly monkey frog (above) has caught a grasshopper with its tongue and is eating the insect. A leopard frog's back legs are much longer than its front legs (right).

kinds live close to the cold
Arctic Circle.

There are three groups of
frogs. Many true frogs, such as
the American bullfrog, live in
North America. They are excel-
lent jumpers. Tree frogs, such
as spring peepers, have sticky
pads on their toes to help
them climb trees. The frogs in
the third group have thicker
skin and spend most of their
lives on dry land. Some people
call this group "toads."

Although the spring peeper (left) is tiny, it whistles loudly for a mate. This Fowler's toad (below) has dry, bumpy skin.

You can think of the word "toad" as a nickname for some kinds of frogs. Before scientists spent much time studying frogs, they called the ones with thin, slippery skin and long back legs "frogs." They called the fat, slow-moving ones with dry, rough skin "toads." Since that time, scientists have learned that some "frogs" are more closely related to "toads" than they are to other "frogs."

a Toad?

Do you think the amphibian below is a frog or a toad? It may look like a frog, but it is a fire-bellied toad.

Silent Salamanders

All salamanders have a long tail, and most have four short, weak legs. Many spend most of their adult lives hidden beneath logs, rocks, and leaves in forests in warm parts of the world. They usually sit in one spot and wait for insects, snails,

The spotted salamander is black with bright yellow or orange spots.

This eastern tiger salamander is eating an earthworm.

and worms to pass by. Salamanders depend on their eyes and their sense of smell to spot a meal.

The enemies of salamanders include raccoons, owls, shrews, snakes, and large frogs. If a salamander's bright colors or bad taste do not scare a predator away, the salamander may use another kind of trick. When an enemy grabs certain kinds of salamanders by the

This salamander has dropped its tail to escape from an enemy. Soon it will grow a new one.

tail, the tail breaks off and keeps wriggling. The hungry predator is distracted by the tail and does not see the sneaky salamander scurry out of sight.

Amphibians in Our Lives

Amphibians play an important role in our lives. They eat many of the insects that harm our crops and spread diseases. In some parts of the world, people eat frog legs. Scientists have found that the liquids produced by some amphibians can

Many people think that frog legs taste like chicken.

be used to make important medicines.

Amphibians have been a part of the world for millions of years, but they are now in

When loggers cut down trees, they may be destroying the homes of some amphibians. A logging truck (left) pulls a full load of newly cut trees that used to be homes for some amphibians. The smoke rising from the smokestacks of this factory (below) contains chemicals that may hurt amphibians.

danger of disappearing forever. Amphibians are very sensitive to changes in their environment. When we pollute the air they breathe and the water they live in, we often kill them. As we fill in wetlands or clear land to build homes, roads, and shopping centers, we destroy the places where amphibians live. We must do whatever we can to protect amphibians. We want them to continue to be part of our world.

To Find Out More

Here are some additional resources to help you learn more about amphibians:

 **Books**

Crewe, Sabrina and Colin Newman. **The Frog.** Raintree Steck-Vaughn, 1997.

Howell, Catherine Herbert. **Reptiles and Amphibians.** National Geographic Society, 1993.

Julivert, Maria Angels. **The Fascinating World of Frogs and Toads**. Barrons Juveniles, 1993.

Kalman, Bobbie and Jacqueline Laguille. **What Is an Amphibian?** Crabtree, 1999.

Martin, James and Art Wolfe. **Frogs.** Crown Publishing, 1997.

Miller, Sara Swan. **Frogs and Toads: The Leggy Leapers.** Franklin Watts, 1999.

_____. **Salamanders: Secret, Silent Lives.** Franklin Watts, 2000.

Organizations and Online Sites

Caecilians Web Site
http://www.peagreenboat.com/eels/

This site features photos and movies of caecilians as well as interesting information about them.

Frogland
http://allaboutfrogs.org

Look here for the frog of the month, interesting trivia about frogs and toads, myths and legends about amphibians, book lists, and lots of links to other sites.

The Legend of the Meeps Island Flying Frog
http://www.amnh.org/ Exhibition/Expedition/ Endangered/meeps/index. html

This story of what it means to be endangered is part of the American Museum of Natural History's website.

Newt and Salamander
http://www.users. interport.net/~spiff/Newt %26Salamander.html

For information about keeping and caring for a newt or salamander, try this site. You'll also find general information about and photos of these curious little creatures as well as links to other sites.

North American Amphibian Monitoring Program
http://www.im.nbs.gov/ amphibs.html

Scientists are worried that amphibians are in danger of vanishing from Earth forever. This site describes the work of scientists who count amphibians and keep track of their activities, so that we can learn more about them.

45

Important Words

caecilian a wormlike amphibian that lives underground

cold blooded having a body temperature that changes as air or water temperature changes

estivate to rest underground during hot, dry weather

gland a part of the body that makes and gives off a chemical substance

hibernate to spend the winter in a resting state

larva the first stage in the life cycle of some animals; plural is larvae

metamorphosis the changes an amphibian goes through to become an adult

predator an animal that kills and eats other animals

Index

Meet the Author

Melissa Stewart earned a Bachelor's Degree in biology from Union College and a Master's Degree in Science and Environmental Journalism from New York University. She has been writing about science and nature for almost a decade. Ms. Stewart lives in Danbury, Connecticut.